WINDY CITY KITCHENS

RECIPES FROM
CHICAGO'S FAVORITE
RESTAURANTS

Dedicated to our little Peanut.

Acknowledgments

Many thanks to the chefs and participating restaurants for their time, enthusiasm and support of the **Windy City Kitchens** cookbook. A collection of favorite recipes and culinary tips can only make better cooks out of us all.

Thanks to Tabulau Tau for the beautiful tableware used throughout the book.

To our graphic design firm, Smith Design, thank you for countless hours of artistic design and creative ideas.

Our photographer, Laurie Proffitt, for capturing the beauty and elegance of our chef's masterful, culinary creations.

Thanks to Sam's Wines & Spirits and particularly wine specialist, Brian Rosen, for a wonderful selection of wine recommendations.

Design: Smith Design

Cover Illustration: Nicholas Wilton

Photography: Proffitt Photography

Wine Pairing: Sam's Wines & Spirits
Specialist Brian Rosen

Culinary/Photography Props: Tabulau Tau

Publisher: Elaine K. Miller

Editor: John W. Miller

Publishing Company:
Eleni Publishing, Inc.

Distributors: Partners Book
Distributing and The Booksource

Copyright © 1997
by Eleni Publishing, Inc.
1835 North Halsted, Suite 1
Chicago, IL 60614
tel: 312.642.7024
fax: 312.266.6328

ISBN: 0-9659678-0-8
Manufactured in the
United States of America

Windy City Kitchens is available at a
special discount when purchased in
bulk for sales promotions as well as
for fund-raising activities. For fur-
ther information, or to order directly,
please contact: Eleni Publishing,
Inc., 1835 North Halsted, Suite 1,
Chicago, IL 60614
tel: 312.642.7024
fax: 312.266.6328

Introduction

Magnificent restaurants are a claim to fame for the city of Chicago. No matter what your taste, Chicago has a restaurant to indulge your pallet. Amazing chefs, exceptional service and elaborate presentations are the calling cards of Chicago's favorite restaurants. Nowhere in the world will you find more diversity and ethnicity available for your dining pleasures.

The compilation of restaurant recipes found in the pages of **Windy City Kitchens** gives readers, culinary experts or otherwise, an opportunity to recreate fine Chicago style dining. The restaurants selected to participate in the cookbook were chosen based upon reviews and rankings in various culinary publications as well as popular opinion of many trusted individuals. It is with great pride that we present to you the **Windy City Kitchens** cookbook. Bon Appetit!

Table of Contents

Appetizer

Entree

Dessert

Arun's   8
Rice Noodles with
Marinated Chicken

Berghoff   10
Roulade of Beef

Bistro 110   12
Tuna "Filet Mignon" with
Wild Mushrooms Sauce

Blue Mesa   14
White Chocolate Quesadilla
with Honey-Raspberry Sauce

Brasserie Jo   16
Braised Lamb Shank
with Garlic

Cafe Absinthe   18
Grilled Ostrich with
Strawberry Red Onion Salad

Cafe Bernard   20
Grilled Portabella
Mushrooms

Cafe Spiaggia   22
Gamberi con Fagiolini

Daniel J's   24
Bread Pudding

Dish   26
Blue Corn Shortcakes
with Berries and
Creme Fraiche

Erwin   28
Bisque of Butternut
Squash with Apple Cider

Everest   30
Cold Terrine of Bouillabaisse

Green Dolphin Street   32
Peppercorn Venison with
Rice and Chutney

Havana   34
Oven Roasted "Jerked" Red
Snapper with a Tomato Mojo

Hudson Club   36
Asian Pear Salad

Kiki's Bistro   38
Poulet Roti

Le Bouchon   40
Onion Tart

Les Nomades   42
Clam Caraway Chowder

Mango   44
Banana Mousse Cake
with Almond Sponge

The Mashed Potato Club   46
Black Bean Hummus

Nick's Fishmarket   48
Crabcakes with Citrus
Beurre Blanc

Papagus   50
Dried Cherry and
Pistachio Baklava

Printer's Row   52
Old Fashioned Apple Tart

Pump Room   54
Crispy Duck with
Braised Red Cabbage

Shaw's Crab House   56
Soft Shell Blue Crab
with Mango

Sole Mio   58
Chocolate Caramel Custard

Soul Kitchen   60
Paella "Jambalaya Style"
in a Spicy Saffron Broth

Starfish   62
Seared Jumbo Scallops
& Vegetable Salad

Topo Gigio   64
Pan Roasted Chilean
Sea Bass

Un Grand Cafe   66
Porcini Crusted Sauteed
Salmon Steak

Vinci   68
Linguine della Nonna

Yoshi's Cafe   70
Veal Chop with Candied
Lemon Zest and Ginger

Restaurant Locations   72

Glossary of Cooking Terms   74

Index   76

Conversion Chart   78

ARUN'S

Located on the north side of Chicago, Arun's serves the city's best traditional Thai cuisine. Executive Chef / Owner Arun Sampanthavivat works magic in the kitchen and goes to extreme measures to pamper dinner guests. Arun's has received numerous culinary awards in its 12-year history. The cuisine is known for the delicacy of its spicing, the care in its presentation, and the continual creation of refined dishes within the ancient traditions of Thai cookery.

Rice Noodles with Marinated Chicken

INGREDIENTS

Chicken Marinade:

1 tsp. corn oil

1 tsp. egg white

1/4 tsp. salt

1/4 tsp. sugar

1/4 tsp. white pepper

1 tsp. corn starch

1 tsp. thin soy sauce

1 tsp. dark soy sauce

1/2 Tbs. finely chopped scallions

1 cup chicken, thinly sliced

Jalapeno vinaigrette sauce:

1 cup vinegar

1 tsp. salt

1 jalapeno pepper, diced

Stir Fry:

1/2 Tbs. garlic, finely minced

3 Tbs. corn oil

3 - 4 cups fresh rice noodles (available in most oriental food stores)

3 Tbs. thin soy sauce

1 Tbs. dark soy sauce

1 Tbs. sugar

1/4 tsp. white pepper

1 cup Shanghai bok choy, 1/2 lengthwise cut

1/4 cup onion, diced

1/4 cup chicken stock

2 eggs

1 cup bean sprouts

Mix marinade ingredients together and refrigerate 20 - 30 minutes prior to cooking.

Mix vinaigrette ingredients together. Set aside.

Brown minced garlic in 2 Tbs. of oil on medium heat. Stir fry marinated chicken into garlic, then add fresh rice noodles, both soy sauces, sugar, and white pepper. Continue to stir fry, adding bok-choy, onion and gradually add chicken stock to soften the noodles and vegetables. Quickly mix ingredients, then push the noodles to the side of pan. Add 1 Tbs. corn oil and turn up heat to high.

Start cooking the eggs on the empty side of the pan. As soon as the egg is relatively set, immediately fold noodles onto the egg. Gently toss all the ingredients together. Then, fold in the bean sprouts with the heat turned-off.

Transfer to serving plates and serve with jalapeno vinaigrette sauce.

SERVES: 2

 Wine Recommendation: Acacia Pinot Noir

Family owned and managed for nearly 100 years, The Berghoff Restaurant is a Chicago tradition and offers a unique dining experience. Located in the heart of Chicago's Loop, The Berghoff has one of the most diverse menus in the city. Chef Matthew Reichel changes the menu frequently and features innovative American cuisine, seafood, salads, and hearty German house specialties. The Berghoff continues to be a favorite destination for generations of diners both locally and internationally.

Roulade of Beef

INGREDIENTS

- 1 Tbs. browning sauce
- 9 cups of beef stock
- 1 bottle of Madeira - sweet fortified wine
- 4 pieces of 6 oz. beef cutlet
- 1/2 lb. of ground veal
- 2 Tbs. garlic, minced
- 1 onion, chopped
- 1 Tbs. marjoram, minced
- 8 celery sticks
- 8 carrot sticks
- 4 pickles
- 2 bay leaves
- 2 Tbs. butter
- 2 Tbs. flour
- salt & pepper to taste

To make the demi-glace, mix browning sauce, 1 cup beef stock and 1 cup Madeira in a saucepan over medium heat. Reduce by half to the proper consistency, which should coat the back of a spoon. Set aside.

Pound the cutlets to uniform thickness, sprinkle with salt & pepper. Set aside. Take the ground veal and mix with garlic, onion and marjoram. Roll each cutlet with ¼ of the ground veal mixture, 2 celery sticks, and 2 carrot sticks, and 1 pickle. Use toothpicks or skewer to hold closed.

Pan sear over high heat. Add 8 cups of beef stock and bay leafs to cover rolled filets and cook until interior temperature reaches 145°.

To make broth, add ½ bottle of Madeira, demi-glace and salt and let simmer for at least 1 hour.

In a separate pan, melt 2 Tbs. butter and gradually stir in 2 Tbs. of flour. Let the roux gently cook until it becomes brownish in color and flour has a chance to cook (do not burn). The roux should have a nutty smell. Remove rolled filets from broth. Set aside. Thicken broth with roux. If necessary, strain sauce to help remove lumps.

Slice cutlets and fan on serving plate. Pour sauce on cutlets and serve.

SERVES: 4

Wine Recommendation: Rodney Strong Crown Cabernet

Bistro 110

Bistro 110 offers an exciting French bistro tradition with an American accent. This Michigan Avenue hot spot specializes in hearty wood-burning oven-roasted cuisine, flavorful pasta, salads, and extraordinary desserts. Executive Chef Dominique Tougne's professional history includes significant periods of study in France with leading figures in French cuisine. Chef Tougne has been able to develop his own signature cuisine based upon the art of presentation, seasoning, and the reinterpretation of classic bistro dishes.

Tuna "Filet Mignon" with Wild Mushrooms Sauce

INGREDIENTS

1 Tbs. balsamic vinegar

¼ tsp. ground coriander

¼ tsp. allspice

⅛ tsp. ground cloves

1 tsp. Worcestershire sauce

5 Tbs. extra virgin olive oil

1 tsp. pink peppercorns

1 Idaho baking potato (about 6 oz.)

3 Tbs. butter

2 Tbs. heavy cream

2 round pieces of yellow-fin tuna (8 oz. each)

6 oz. mixed mushrooms (such as oyster, crimini, portabella)

salt & pepper to taste

parsley to garnish

Preheat oven to 400°.

Combine the balsamic vinegar, coriander, allspice, cloves, Worcestershire sauce, and salt & pepper. Mix well. Slowly add 3½ Tbs. olive oil and pink peppercorns. Set aside.

Bring water to boil in a small saucepan. Peel potato and chop into small chunks. Add potatoes to boiling water with salt. Simmer until tender (6-8 minutes). Drain, allow potatoes to dry briefly. In a mixer, add potatoes, butter, heavy cream, salt and pepper. Mix until smooth, and set aside.

Season the tuna with salt and pepper. Lightly coat the bottom of a heavy, oven-proof frying pan with 1 Tbs. olive oil. Heat the pan until nearly smoking. Sear tuna for 2 minutes on each side. Transfer to the oven and cook an additional 4 minutes to medium-rare.

Clean the mushrooms, trim the stems and cut into chunks. Lightly toss the mushrooms with remaining olive oil, season with salt and pepper, and roast in oven for 10 minutes or until softened.

Portion the tuna onto warm plates with the mushrooms and mashed potatoes. Spoon the balsamic sauce over tuna. Garnish with parsley.

SERVES: 2

 Wine Recommendation: Grgich Hills Chardonnay

Blue Mesa brings Santa Fe to Chicago. Located in Lincoln Park's Theater District, Blue Mesa serves authentic Southwestern and New Mexican cuisine. The restaurant's warm and colorful surroundings offer a true representation of New Mexican design. The pueblo-style interior, complete with white stucco walls, kiva fireplaces, and stylish regional art, pays tribute to the Southwestern culture.

White Chocolate Quesadilla With Honey-Raspberry Sauce

INGREDIENTS

10 oz. frozen raspberries

4 oz. honey

2 oz. raspberry liqueur

6 flour tortillas, quartered (8 inches)

1 cup cinnamon-sugar

vegetable oil

8 oz. white chocolate, coarsely chopped

4 Tbs. sweet butter

2 eggs, separated and at room temperature

pinch of salt

pinch of cream of tartar

1/4 cup sugar

1/4 cup heavy cream

1 tsp. vanilla

powdered sugar

sprig of mint

To prepare sauce, combine raspberries, honey and liqueur in a blender. Blend, strain and set aside until serving. To make the sauce sweeter, add more honey.

Fry tortillas in vegetable oil in a saute pan over medium heat until crisp. Coat with cinnamon-sugar. Set aside.

To prepare mousse, melt chocolate pieces and butter in the top of a double-boiler over barely simmering water. Stir until smooth. Transfer to a medium bowl. Quickly whisk in egg yolks one at a time.

In a separate bowl, beat the egg whites with salt and cream of tartar at medium speed until frothy.

Begin beating egg whites at high speed, gradually adding 2 Tbs. sugar. Beat until stiff, but not dry.

Beat cream with remaining sugar and vanilla until slightly thickened. Fold egg whites and whipped cream into the chocolate and chill, covered, for 4 hours.

To prepare quesadillas, spread mousse between 2 flour tortillas like a sandwich. Sprinkle with powdered sugar and place on dessert plates with points facing each other. Spoon raspberry sauce on each side. Garnish with a sprig of mint in the center.

SERVES: 6

 Wine Recommendation: Columbia Crest Semillon

Brasserie Joe offers an authentic European dining experience with a more casual approach. The restaurant features wholesome, comforting Alsace cuisine, as well as its own Alsace-style draft beer and an extensive selection of French wines. Brasserie Joe and Chef-Owner Jean Joho have won numerous culinary awards, including the coveted James Beard Foundation Award for best new restaurant. Chef Joho has created his authentic menu from family recipes and the culinary heritage of France.

Braised Lamb Shank with Garlic

INGREDIENTS

4 medium-sized lamb shanks, trimmed well

3 Tbs. olive oil

20 garlic cloves, unpeeled

1 tsp. of the combined chopped herbs (thyme, rosemary, sage and basil)

1 cup Alsace Riesling (dry, aromatic wine)

2 cups cooked French flageolets (a delicate kind of bean, may be substituted with navy or pea beans)

1 cup French string beans

salt & pepper to taste

Preheat oven to 350°. In a roasting pan, brown the shanks, season with salt, pepper and olive oil. Add the garlic and cook in oven for ½ hour.

Add the chopped herbs, white wine and braise for approximately 1½ hours. Be sure to leave the lid on the roasting pan for ¾ of the cooking time.

When the liquid is reduced to a quarter of the volume, add the cooked flageolets, and string beans and cook for another 20 minutes.

In a well heated dish, serve the lamb shank whole to your guest. On the side, serve mashed potatoes with sauted shallots.

SERVES: 4

 Wine Recommendation: Fess Parker Syrah

Cafe Absinthe

Located in the heart of Chicago's trendy Bucktown neighborhood, Cafe Absinthe serves up creative bistro-style cooking with lots of attitude. Dark, funky and noisy, Cafe Absinthe exudes the atmosphere of an old world Absinthe House and showcases a mysterious alley entrance. Executive Chef Joshua Young changes the menu daily and treats dinner guests to a truly memorable evening.

Grilled Ostrich with Strawberry Red Onion Salad

INGREDIENTS

Strawberry Red Onion Salad:

2 Tbs. raspberry vinegar

1 Tbs. balsamic vinegar

½ bunch cilantro, medium-chopped

½ tsp. cheyenne pepper

1 tsp. sugar

3 pints red strawberries, quartered and hulled

½ red onion small

salt & pepper to taste

Creme Fraiche:

8 Tbs. creme fraiche

1 Tbs. toasted & ground fresh cumin seed

salt & pepper to taste

four 3 oz. portions of ostrich filet

Garnish:

fried tortilla strips

For the strawberry salad, combine vinegars, cilantro, cheyenne pepper, sugar, salt & pepper. Add strawberries and red onion and marinate for 2 - 4 hours.

For creme fraiche, fold toasted cumin seeds into creme fraiche and season with salt & pepper. Set aside.

Grill the ostrich for 2 minutes on all sides. Season liberally with salt & pepper.

Place strawberry salad on serving plate. Sprinkle creme fraiche on top of salad. Place the ostrich on top of the salad, garnish with fried tortilla strips, and serve.

SERVES: 4

Wine Recommendation: Foxen Pinot Noir

CAFE BERNARD

A Lincoln Park mainstay for over 25 years, Cafe Bernard serves exquisite French cuisine. The atmosphere is romantically intimate with a comfortable bistro feel. Executive Chef / Owner Bernard Lecoq continues to impress his diners with a frequently changing menu, as well as many house specialties.

Grilled Portabella Mushrooms

INGREDIENTS

2 medium garlic cloves, peeled and crushed

4 Tbs. extra virgin olive oil

1 large sprig thyme (stems removed), finely chopped

½ bay leaf, crushed

2 medium portabella mushroom caps (each about 4 inches wide)

6 pieces (halves) dried tomatoes

½ shallot, finely diced

pinch of salt

2 cups fresh spinach leaves, packed

1 (4 oz.) fresh goat cheese log (French chevre or domestic), sliced in half and flattened

3 Tbs. balsamic vinegar

paprika (optional)

In a shallow glass dish, combine garlic, 1½ Tbs. olive oil, thyme and bay leaf. Add mushroom caps. Cover and refrigerate for 6 hours.

Soak dried tomatoes in 1 part olive oil/3 parts warm water for 2 hours, drain. Set aside.

Drain mushrooms and slice them ½ inch thick on the bias. In a very hot, medium-size skillet, sear mushrooms in some olive oil from the marinade for 30 to 45 seconds total, turning once. Then grill mushrooms briefly to create decorative grill marks, or broil the mushrooms until lightly browned and slightly crunchy. Set skillet aside for vinaigrette.

Heat a second medium skillet until very hot. Add 1 tsp. olive oil. When oil starts to smoke, stir in shallots, dried tomatoes and salt. Add spinach and toss quickly. Remove from heat. Meanwhile, warm goat cheese on a heat-safe plate in a pre-heated 350° oven until soft, but not melted (about 90 seconds.)

Place spinach mixture in the center of 2 plates. Top with mushroom slices.

Heat the vinegar and 1½ tsp. olive oil in the first skillet over medium heat, stirring with a fork and scraping up any crusty bits of mushroom from bottom of pan. When warm, drizzle over mushrooms and spinach.

Top each serving with a round of warmed goat cheese. Sprinkle with paprika if desired. Serve warm.

SERVES: 2

Wine Recommendation: Gundlach-Bundschu Merlot

Cafe Spiaggia

Cafe Spiaggia is an elegantly casual and contemporary dining experience located in the heart of Michigan Avenue. Award-winning Executive Chef Paul Bartolotta is internationally acclaimed for his innovation, excellence and passion for preparing Italian cuisine. Vibrant scents and endearing flavors are the signatures of Chef Bartolotta's cuisine and his menus are a celebration of simplicity and the changing seasons.

Gamberi con Fagiolini

INGREDIENTS

- 1 egg yolk
- 1 Tbs. mustard
- ³/₄ tsp. salt
- ¹/₈ tsp. white pepper
- ¹/₂ cup corn oil
- ¹/₂ cup & 6 Tbs. extra virgin olive oil
- 2 Tbs. lemon juice
- 2 tsp. brandy
- 2 Tbs. water
- 2 quarts water
- ¹/₂ lb. tiny string beans (or haricot vert)
- 12 pieces of shrimp, peeled & deveined
- ¹/₄ cup diced tomato (no seeds)
- ¹/₈ tsp. fresh ground pepper
- 4 flat basil sprigs

In an electric mixer, place egg yolk, mustard, ¼ tsp. salt and white pepper. Whip over medium speed. Slowly drizzle in corn oil until finished, followed by ½ cup olive oil. Reduce speed to low, add lemon juice, brandy and 2 Tbs. water (which will dilute the mayonnaise to a thin pourable consistency). Set aside.

Bring 2 quarts of water to a rolling boil, season with ¼ tsp. of salt. Trim ends of tiny string beans. Cut beans in approximately 1-inch lengths and cook in boiling water for 4-5 minutes or until tender-crisp, but not crunchy. Remove with a slotted spoon and place in a mixing bowl.

In the same water, boil the shrimp for 4-5 minutes. While shrimp are cooking, add tomatoes, ¼ tsp. salt, fresh ground pepper, and 2 Tbs. olive oil to beans.

Place equal portions of the bean mix on 4 small plates. Place 3 cooked shrimp on top of the beans. Drizzle the shrimp and beans with 1 Tbs. of the brandy mayonnaise. Also drizzle each with 1 Tbs. olive oil and garnish with sprig of basil.

SERVES: 4

 Wine Recommendation: Robert Mondavi Coastal Chardonnay

Daniel J's

A north side Chicago legend, Daniel J's serves eclectic American cuisine with a hint of Mediterranean influence. The atmosphere is casual, and the storefront setting is comfortably crowded. Executive Chef / Owner Jack Jones creates marvelous cuisine with creativity, passion, and a dedication to serving bold plates.

Bread Pudding

INGREDIENTS

1/2 stick butter (softened)

1 loaf white bread (25 slices)

5 cups whole milk

6 whole eggs

5 egg yolks

1 3/4 cups sugar

3 Tbs. kahlua

3 Tbs. amaretto

5 Tbs. real vanilla extract

Caramel:

1/4 lb. butter

1/2 tsp. lemon juice

3 cups sugar

1 1/2 cups heavy whipping cream

Preheat oven to 275°.

Butter and toast the bread. Trim off crusts, and cut slices into triangles. Line a 9 x 2 inch round pie pan with the points up.

Boil the milk. In a mixer combine all the eggs and yolks with the sugar, kahlua, amaretto, vanilla and the milk. Be sure to mix well. Skim off any foam.

Pour the "custard" mixture into the bread-lined pan. Prepare a water bath by pouring hot or simmering water in a roasting pan and then place the bread pudding pan into the water bath. Don't let the water spill into the pie pan.

Bake the bread pudding in the water bath at 275° for 55 to 60 minutes or until just firm. Let cool.

Prepare the caramel by slowly cooking 1/4 lb. butter, 1/2 tsp. lemon juice, and 3 cups sugar in a big, deep saucepan until it turns to a brownish color. Remove from heat and stir in the 1 1/2 cups of heavy whipping cream.

Drizzle warm caramel sauce over slices of the bread pudding and serve.

SERVES: 8

Wine Recommendation: Robert Pecota Muscato di Andrea

24

Located in Chicago's Wrigleyville neighborhood, Dish serves American cuisine influenced by the Southwest. Executive Chef / Owner Patrick O'Dea oversees an ever-evolving menu inspired by seasonally available produce. Dish has received high marks from many leading culinary publications and continues to dazzle its patrons.

Blue Corn Shortcakes with Berries and Creme Fraiche

INGREDIENTS

¹/₂ pint (each) raspberries, blueberries and sliced strawberries

¹/₂ cup + 1 Tbs. sugar

³/₄ cup champagne

2 cups Bisquick

1 cup blue cornmeal

pinch baking powder

pinch salt

1 cup buttermilk

¹/₂ stick melted butter

6 Tbs. creme fraiche

Preheat oven to 425°.

In large non-reactive bowl (glass or porcelain) combine berries and 1 Tbs. sugar. Toss until sugar-coated. Add champagne and set in refrigerator for at least 1-2 hours (the longer the better).

In large bowl, sift together Bisquick, blue corn meal, sugar, baking powder, and salt. When well-mixed, slowly add buttermilk—the batter should hold together loosely.

Spoon onto non-greased cookie sheet. Bake 8-10 minutes. Remove from oven and baste with melted butter. Continue cooking 4-5 minutes more or until well-golden blue. More basting will ensure a better color.

Remove shortcakes from sheet immediately and place on cooling rack. When cool, slice in half and fill with a spoonful of creme fraiche and champagned berry mix. Replace top and add more creme and berries.

SERVES: 6

 Wine Recommendation: Girard Dry Chenin Blanc

erwin

Located in Chicago's Lake View neighborhood, Erwin, an American cafe, pampers its guests with urban heartland cuisine. Executive Chef/Owner Erwin Drechsler and wife Cathy utilize the freshest seasonal ingredients available, primarily drawing from the Midwest region. Chef Erwin's cooking techniques are drawn from French cooking traditions, yet the outcome is uniquely American. Nationally acclaimed, Erwin continues to provide exceptional service and personal attention that makes for a wonderfully relaxing evening.

Bisque of Butternut Squash with Apple Cider

INGREDIENTS

1 Tbs. butter

2 carrots, peeled & diced

2 celery stalks, diced

2 yellow onions, diced

3 peeled, cored & diced Granny Smith apples

8 cups peeled butternut squash, diced

12 cups seasoned chicken stock

1 tsp. cinnamon

1 tsp. ground nutmeg

3 Tbs. brown sugar

2 cups (or more) apple cider

sour cream

thin slices of Granny Smith apple

Melt butter in a large stockpot with a cover. Add carrots, celery, onions, apples and squash. Steam vegetables and fruit, covered, over low heat for 20 minutes.

Heat stock in a separate pan. Add simmering stock to vegetables and continue to cook over medium heat, uncovered until butternut squash is soft. Whisk in cinnamon, nutmeg, brown sugar and apple cider.

Lower heat and simmer for 1 hour. Puree soup in batches in blender or food processor.

Reheat to serve. Serve with a dollop of sour cream and thin slices of Granny Smith apples.

SERVES: 12

 Wine Recommendation: Chateau St. Michelle Dry Riesling

erwin

Floating atop the Chicago skyline, Everest and Chef-Owner Jean Joho dazzle guests with personalized French cuisine. Chef Jean Joho has been honored by the acclaimed James Beard Foundation as best chef in the Midwest and Everest has received 4-star reviews from the *Chicago Tribune*, *Chicago Sun-Times* and *Chicago Magazine*. Everest has also received the AAA 5-diamond award as well as the Mobil Travel Guide 5-star award. Chef Joho's light cooking style is characterized by fresh seasonal American ingredients and the creative presentation of each signature dish.

Cold Terrine of Bouillabaisse

INGREDIENTS

1 leek

¹/₄ cup olive oil

4 garlic cloves, peeled and minced

1 onion, peeled and chopped

1 medium carrot, diced

1 fennel bulb, sliced

2 tomatoes, diced

1 cup fish stock or 1 cup of clam juice

¹/₂ tsp. saffron twigs

2 springs thyme, minced

1 tsp. salt

¹/₄ tsp. cayenne pepper

¹/₂ lb. monk fish (cut in 1¹/₂ inch cubes)

¹/₂ lb. sea bass (cut in 1¹/₂ inch cubes)

¹/₂ lb. red snapper (cut in 1¹/₂ inch cubes)

¹/₂ lb. sea scallops (cut in 1¹/₂ inch cubes)

¹/₂ lb. medium shrimp, peeled and deveined

6 gelatin leaves

Cut off green tops of leek and trim the root end. Wash and boil leek until tender in salted water. Shock in ice water and dry. Layer terrine with cooked leaves and set aside.

In a large non-aluminum stock pot, heat olive oil over medium to high heat, saute the garlic, onion, carrot and fennel until soft (about 7 minutes).

Stir in the tomatoes, reduce heat slightly and cook for another 5 minutes. Pour in the fish stock or clam juice, add saffron, thyme, salt and cayenne pepper and bring to a boil over high heat. Add monk fish and cook 2 minutes, then stir in the rest of the fish and shellfish. Reduce heat to medium-high and cook for approximately 4 minutes or until the fish is cooked through, but not flaking apart.

Remove fish and vegetables from fish stock and ladle into the terrine. Dissolve the gelatin in warm fish stock and strain over the ingredients in the terrine. Wrap with the rest of the leek and refrigerate for 12 hours.

For serving, slice terrine and present with a mesclun and fennel salad. You can substitute whatever fish is available.

SERVES: 8

 Wine Recommendation: Alsace Albrecht Riesling

green DOLPHIN street

Bucktown meets Lincoln Park. The owners of the Green Dolphin Street restaurant converted a junkyard and auto-glass repair shop into a stunning restaurant and jazz club. The restaurant serves uncompromising contemporary American fare under the watchful eye of Executive Chef Victor Gechrit. Many dinner guests enjoy a truly memorable meal and end the evening listening to a set of live jazz in the cabaret room.

Peppercorn Venison with Rice and Chutney

INGREDIENTS

Venison:

2 lbs. venison chop (8 oz. per chop)

1/4 cup chopped garlic

1/8 cup chopped rosemary

black pepper to season

2 Tbs. olive oil

Rice:

1 cup mirepoix (chopped onion, carrot, celery)

2 cups jasmine rice

1/4 cup white wine

2 cups chicken stock

1/2 cup currants

1/2 cup total of parmesan, asiago, and mascarpone cheese

Peppercorn Sauce:

1 Tbs. green peppercorns

3/4 cup white wine

3 cups veal stock

3 Tbs. honey

Chutney:

1 1/2 cup red wine

1 cup red wine vinegar

1/2 cup chopped onions

1 cup diced rhubarb

1 cup diced pear

1 cup water

cheesecloth spice bag containing: cinnamon stick, star anise, fresh thyme, white peppercorns, whole allspice, juniper, berries, cloves, and cardamo

Combine venison, garlic, rosemary, and black pepper and marinate for 1½ days.

Saute mirepoix. Add rice and white wine. Reduce by ½ the liquid. Add chicken stock. Cook until rice is tender. Add currants and cheese. Let stand and cool. Remove mirepoix.

Combine green peppercorns with white wine and heat in a sauce pan. Reduce by ½ the liquid. Add veal stock and honey. Reduce until sauce consistency. Set aside.

Combine red wine, vinegar, onions and spice bag and heat in a sauce pan. Reduce by ¾ the liquid. Add rhubarb, pear and 1 cup water. Cook until tender. Set aside.

Heat 2 Tbs. olive oil in large skillet and brown venison on all sides over medium-high heat, about 3-4 minutes per side. Do not overcook. Venison should be medium-rare to medium.

Warm rice. Set rice, chutney and venison on serving plate. Drizzle peppercorn sauce over venison.

SERVES: 4

 Wine Recommendation: Caymus Cabernet

*Recipe provided by Chef Marshall Blair

Located in Chicago's River North area, Havana serves authentic Cuban cuisine with adventurous attitude. Executive Chef Philip Butler combines the simple roots of traditional Cuban cooking style with a passion for serving fresh whole fish. The restaurant's atmosphere is that of a classic Cuban cafe with high ceilings, an open kitchen, and many unique Cuban photographs.

Oven Roasted "Jerked" Red Snapper with a Tomato Mojo

INGREDIENTS

Jerk Marinade:

3 Tbs. crushed red pepper

20 cachucha peppers, stems removed

1 onion, peeled and chopped

1 cup parsley, chopped

2 Tbs. ginger, peeled and chopped

3 1/2 Tbs. salt, to taste

3 tsp. fresh thyme, chopped

1 Tbs. black pepper, ground

1/2 tsp. nutmeg, ground

1/8 tsp. cloves, ground

1/4 cup lime juice

3 Tbs. soy sauce

4 Tbs. vegetable oil

1 Tbs. brown sugar

Red Snapper:

1 1/2 - 2 lb. red snapper, dressed

3 Tbs. vegetable oil

Salsa:

30 cachucha peppers, stems removed

4 each roma tomatoes, seeded and diced

1/4 cup red onion, peeled and diced

2 cloves garlic, minced

1 pinch cumin, ground

2 Tbs. cilantro, chopped

3 jalapeno peppers, minced (optional)

Mojo:

1/4 cup lime juice

1/2 cup olive oil

1/4 cup onion, minced

1 Tbs. tomato paste

1/2 Tbs. dried oregano

1 tsp. black pepper, ground

To prepare the jerk marinade, puree all marinade ingredients in a food processor until smooth, adding water as needed. Clean the red snapper under cold water. Remove the gills. Make three 1/4" deep slits vertically down each side of the fish. Rub the jerk marinade into the fish and its inner cavity. Refrigerate for 2 hours.

Heat a large saute pan and add 3 Tbs. of oil. Cook fish in oil for 1 minute on each side, then cook in a 400° oven for 8 minutes or until done. Place fish on a serving platter.

To prepare the mojo, mix salsa ingredients. Add the lime juice, olive oil, onion, tomato paste, oregano, and black pepper into a blender with the salsa. Blend for 20 seconds. Add salt to taste. Drizzle mojo sauce over "jerked" red snapper and serve.

SERVES: 2

Wine Recommendation: Marietta Old Vine Red

HUDSON CLUB

The Hudson Club is one of River West's most prized additions. The clientele ranges from local celebrities and sports personalities to Chicago artists and business professionals. The restaurant is located in a turn of the century building and has a fondness for rich velvets, deep woods, brushed aluminum, and futuristic light designs to create a 1940's style supper club. The Hudson Club and Executive Chef Paul Larson offer a menu of eclectic American cuisine with Asian and French influences.

Asian Pear Salad

INGREDIENTS

2 heads baby frisse lettuce

½ cup walnut halves

½ cup sugar

1 Tbs. sherry wine vinegar

1 cup rice wine vinegar

2 cups vegetable oil

4 oz. blue cheese (maytag farms)

2 Asian pears

salt to taste

white pepper to taste

chopped chives to garnish

Cut and wash lettuce and cover with a moist towel in refrigerator until ready to mix.

In a food processor or blender, add ¼ cup of the walnuts, sugar and vinegars. Process until smooth. In a slow and steady stream add the oil to the mixture while the machine is running. Season to taste with salt and white pepper. The vinaigrette can be made and stored in the refrigerator for up to 7 days.

In a large mixing bowl, toss the lettuce with the walnut vinaigrette until the lettuce is coated well. Arrange the lettuce on salad plates. Sprinkle the salads with the remaining ¼ cup of walnuts, blue cheese and chopped chives. Remove the seeds from the pears and slice.

Place the pears in the center of the salad and serve. Once you slice the pears, they will begin to turn brown. Toss the pears lightly with some of the vinaigrette to prolong the color.

SERVES: 4

Wine Recommendation: Havens Sauvignon Blanc

Kiki's Bistro, located on the near north side of Chicago, serves classic French cuisine with a country bistro attitude. The restaurant is pleasantly comfortable with fresh cut flowers, hardwood floors, and an experienced staff to answer any questions. Owner Georges "Kiki" Cuisance and Executive Chef Michael Gregson prepare menus that delight the cosmopolitan crowd. Rumor has it that Kiki's Bistro is the place Chicago chefs dine on their days off.

Poulet Roti

INGREDIENTS

2 lbs. roasted chicken bones

1 carrot, chopped

2 celery stalks, chopped

1 onion, chopped

2 tomatoes, chopped

2 bay leaves

1/2 Tbs. thyme

1 Tbs. peppercorns

2 Tbs. garlic puree

3 cups white wine

6 to 8 cups chicken or veal stock

1 whole chicken Fryer's, 1/2 per person

4 tsp. Herb's d'Provence (wild thyme, rosemary, oregano, basil, marjoram, savory)

4 garlic cloves, pureed

2 tsp. fresh cracked black pepper

2 oz. olive oil

To make chicken jus, place roasted bones in large saucepot. Add vegetables, tomatoes, bay leaves, thyme, peppercorns and 2 Tbs. garlic puree. Add wine and reduce all the way, then add stock. Bring to a boil, then simmer and reduce to sauce consistency. Strain and season to taste with salt. Set aside.

Trim chicken of excess fat. One to two days in advance of serving, marinate the chickens with herb's d' provence, garlic cloves, black pepper and olive oil and keep in refrigerator.

When ready to serve, season with salt, and brown all sides of chicken in a hot saute pan.

Finish roasting in a 400° oven for about 45 minutes. Remove from oven when cooked and allow to rest for 15 minutes before cutting.

Place chicken on serving plate and ladle with chicken jus. Serve with vegetables and mashed potatoes.

SERVES: 2

 Wine Recommendation: St. Clement Chardonnay   *Recipe provided by Chef John Hogan

A Bucktown favorite, Le Bouchon serves traditional French cuisine with a Lyonnaise influence. Executive Chef / Owner Jean Claude Poilevey amazes guests with simple and flavorful dishes, served in a lively and bustling Parisian bistro setting. Le Bouchon regulars adore the small tables, fresh cut flowers and skillfully prepared cuisine.

Onion Tart

INGREDIENTS

Savory Tart Crust:

3 cups all-purpose flour

¼ tsp. salt

1½ sticks unsalted butter

1 cup lukewarm water

Tart Filling:

2 large onions, sliced thin

2 strips bacon

½ cup grated Swiss cheese

1 egg yolk

½ cup heavy cream

pinch of ground nutmeg

salt & pepper to taste

Add salt to flour in a large mixing bowl of a stand mixer. With mixer on slow speed, slowly add butter to flour. Continue mixing until flour resembles course meal.

With mixer on medium speed, add water slowly until dough sticks and dry flour is not visible. Remove dough and shape into a ball. Wrap in cloth and set aside for ½ hour.

Flour working area and rolling pin. Cut dough in ½. Place ½ in freezer for another occasion. Roll the other half into a very thin circle. Allow 2 inches of excess to overhang your tart pan, and press into corners and sides. Cut away excess crust. Using a circle of parchment paper, line inside of crust and weight with pie weights.

Bake crust on sheet pan in 350° oven for 30 minutes. Remove weights and parchment so crust can be filled.

Render fat from bacon in heavy saute pan. When bacon begins to brown, add onions and saute until onions brown, about 10 minutes. Remove bacon and strain onions in colander, stirring occasionally to cool and strain. Don't be concerned if no excess fat strains away.

In a large mixing bowl, whisk egg yolk into cream. Add salt, pepper and nutmeg to taste. Fold in cheese and onions and spoon into crust.

Bake on sheet pan at 375° for about 30 minutes, until tart is brown on top. Remove from oven and cool slightly before cutting.

SERVES: 4-6

 Wine Recommendation: Bonny Doon Vin Gris "Dry Rose"

Les Nomades

The three-story Brownstone which houses Les Nomades is over 110 years old. This once-private club recently opened its doors to the public and serves innovative French cuisine in an intimate Parisian setting. Executive Chef Christopher Koetke continually challenges himself and his staff with a creative and balanced menu that changes daily.

Clam Caraway Chowder

INGREDIENTS

16 cherrystone clams, washed

1 tsp. caraway seed

1 cup chicken stock or low-sodium broth

1½ cup water

4 strips of bacon, chopped finely

½ cup onion, finely chopped

½ cup celery, finely chopped

1 clove of garlic, finely chopped

⅓ cup flour

1 cup cream

2 cups milk

1 bay leaf

1 tsp. thyme

1½ cup potato, diced

salt & pepper to taste

Place the clams, caraway, stock and water in a large covered saucepan. Bring to a boil and simmer for 20 minutes, or until the clams open.

Remove the clams and strain the clam juice. Reserve the clam juice. Chop the clam meat as finely as possible. Set aside.

In a large saucepan, gently cook the bacon, onions and celery until soft. Add the garlic and cook 1 minute. Add the flour and cook 1 more minute. Add the cream and milk and bring to a boil, stirring frequently. Cook until thickened.

Add the clam juice, bay leaf, thyme, and potatoes to the saucepan. Simmer for about 20 minutes or until the potatoes are soft. Add chopped clam meat.

Season to taste with salt and white pepper and serve.

SERVES: 8

 Wine Recommendation: Phelps Gewurztraminer

A River North treasure, Mango offers an American menu with French and Italian influences. Award-winning Executive Chef and Co-owner, Steven Chiappetti prepares cuisine with genuine imagination and presentation. The ambiance is that of an American bistro, pleasantly noisy with plenty of energy. Polished marble and custom-made glass scones in the shape of mangos accent the decor of this popular eatery.

Banana Mousse Cake with Almond Sponge

INGREDIENTS

Saffron Genoise (Sponge Cake):

5 oz. butter

½ tsp. saffron

9 eggs

1½ cups sugar

2 cups flour

Dacqoise (Almond Sponge):

10 oz. almond flour

11 oz. powdered sugar

12 oz. egg whites

1 oz. lemon juice

4 oz. granulated sugar

vegetable spray

Feulliuetine Layer:

14 oz. feulliuetine flakes (Kellogg's rice crispies may be substituted)

12 oz. praline paste

Banana Mousse:

15 oz. banana puree

1½ oz. lemon juice

1½ oz. rum

9 oz. sugar

6 oz. water

9 oz. egg whites

2 sheets bloomed gelatin

Preheat oven to 400°.

To prepare the genoise, place butter and saffron in a microwavable dish and microwave on high until melted.

Place eggs into a bowl and beat on high with ½ of the sugar until pale and lemon colored. Slowly incorporate flour and balance of sugar.

Take some batter and place into the butter and saffron mixture. Fold until the batter is absorbed, then fold into the rest of the batter. Spread batter onto a sheet pan and bake until it springs back roughly 30 - 40 minutes. Cool on a rack.

To prepare the dacquoise, line a sheet pan with parchment paper and lightly grease with vegetable spray. In a mixing bowl, combine flour and powdered sugar. Beat egg whites with lemon juice and ⅓ of the granulated sugar until soft peaks form. Add remaining sugar and beat until stiff peaks form. Gently fold the egg whites to the flour mixture. Spread on the sheet pan and bake for 20 minutes or until golden brown. Cool.

 Wine Recommendation: Scharffeuberger Cremant

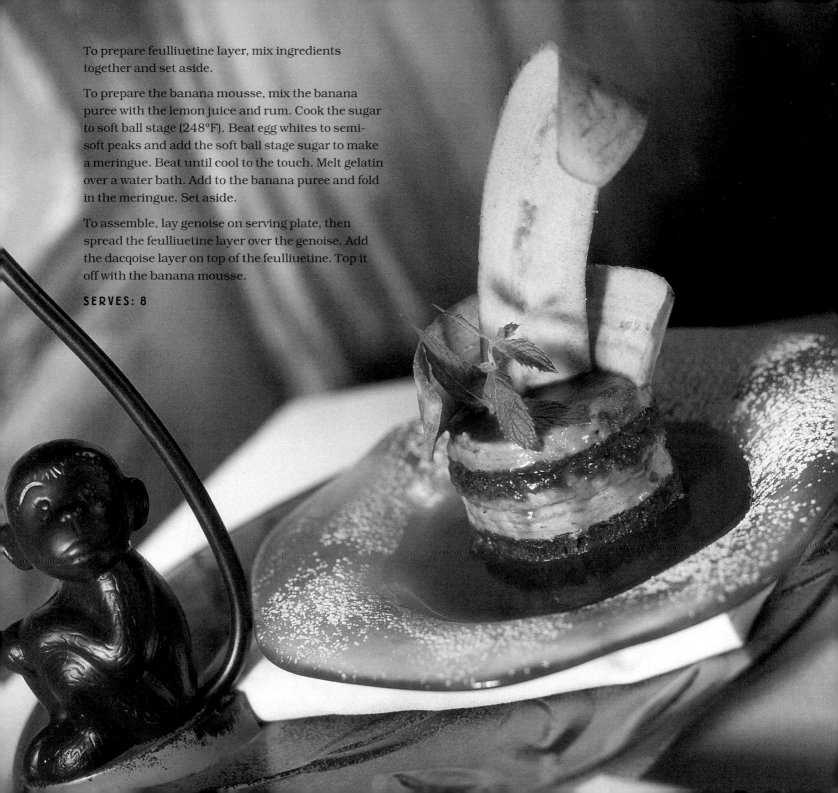

To prepare feulliuetine layer, mix ingredients together and set aside.

To prepare the banana mousse, mix the banana puree with the lemon juice and rum. Cook the sugar to soft ball stage (248°F). Beat egg whites to semi-soft peaks and add the soft ball stage sugar to make a meringue. Beat until cool to the touch. Melt gelatin over a water bath. Add to the banana puree and fold in the meringue. Set aside.

To assemble, lay genoise on serving plate, then spread the feulliuetine layer over the genoise. Add the dacqoise layer on top of the feulliuetine. Top it off with the banana mousse.

SERVES: 8

the Mashed Potato Club

The Mashed Potato Club is described by many as an eccentric and eclectic restaurant. Painted bright yellow on the outside, and decorated with a medley of music and colors inside, The Mashed Potato Club attracts a diverse clientele. The menu is consistently heralded for its simple "home-cooked" favorites all served alongside namesake spuds. Guests can top their spuds with anything from the traditional gravy to the extraordinary, such as caviar and snails. The Mashed Potato Club is truly an experience.

Black Bean Hummus

INGREDIENTS

2¹/₂ lbs. black beans, uncooked

4 qts. water

2¹/₂ Tbs. cumin

1 Tbs. onion powder

1 cup tahini

¹/₃ cup garlic, roasted and pureed

3 Tbs. lemon juice, bottled

1 cup olive oil

1¹/₂ Tbs. salt

1 Tbs. pepper, black ground coarse

Spread the uncooked beans on a sheet pan and pick through them, removing any stones or other foreign objects. Place beans in bowl with cold water to cover and soak overnight.

Drain beans, and cook in 4 qts. water over high heat for 45 minutes or until tender. Drain beans. Set aside and keep warm.

Place warm beans in food processor. Blend until beans are a rough paste. Add cumin, onion powder, tahini, garlic, and lemon juice. Blend until spices are incorporated.

Slowly add olive oil. Blend until a smooth paste is achieved. Season with salt and pepper.

Transfer to a plastic 4-qt. storage container. Place in an ice bath to speed the cooling process. Wrap, label, date and refrigerate.

To serve, scoop hummus with ice cream scoop and place in round red cabbage leaf. Serve with toasted garlic bread, and garnish with lemon and tomato salsa.

SERVES: 2 QUARTS

 Wine Recommendation: Rutherford Hill Merlot

NICK'S FISHMARKET

Located in the center of Chicago's business district, Nick's Fishmarket's intimate but bold atmosphere makes it a perfect setting for business or pleasure. The menu features fresh seafood, but also offers a wide selection of prime beef, veal and pasta. The service is impeccable and Executive Chef Jorg Limper's presentation is not to be forgotten.

Crabcakes with Citrus Beurre Blanc

INGREDIENTS

8 oz. fresh lump crabmeat

1 oz. red bell pepper

1 oz. green bell pepper

1/2 tsp. Coleman's dry mustard

2 Tbs. mayonnaise

1 egg

1/2 cup breadcrumbs (plain white)

1/2 cup additional breadcrumbs to coat patties

4 oz. butter or oil

Citrus Beurre Blanc:

2 cups white wine

1/4 cup lemon juice

1 cup fish stock

1 Tbs. shallots, minced

1/2 bay leaf

1 Tbs. mixed herbs (dill, cilantro, basil, chives) chopped fine

1 1/2 cups 40% whipping cream

Zest of 1 orange

Zest of 1 lime

1 lb. salted butter, room temp.

Salt and white pepper to taste

Finely chop the crabmeat, red and green bell peppers. Combine the crabmeat, red bell peppers, green bell peppers, dry mustard, mayonnaise, egg, 1/2 cup breadcrumbs, and salt & pepper.

Form into four 3 oz. patties (about 3/4 inch high and 3 inches across). Coat lightly with 1/2 cup additional breadcrumbs.

Saute in non-stick skillet with butter or oil until golden brown on each side, about 4 minutes per side.

Combine white wine, lemon juice, fish stock, shallots, bay leaf, herbs, salt and white pepper in a large saucepan. Bring to a boil and reduce by half. Add cream to wine reduction. Bring to a boil and reduce by half.

Remove from heat and stir in butter with whip. Make sure mixture does not become cold while adding butter or it will break. Strain sauce through a cheesecloth. Add lemon and orange zest. Serve at once with crab cakes.

SERVES: 4

 Wine Recommendation: De Loach Chardonnay

PAPAGUS

GREEK TAVERNA

Dried Cherry and Pistachio Baklava

INGREDIENTS

11 oz. pistachios, roughly chopped

5 oz. dried cherries

2 oz. granulated sugar

2 oz. egg yolks

9 sheets phyllo dough

1/2 cup melted butter

Syrup:

1 cup sugar

1 cup water

6 sprigs mint

18 dried cherries (cut in 1/2)

Preheat oven to 350°.

To prepare the filling, combine pistachios, cherries, sugar and egg yolks in a medium-sized bowl and mix well. Set aside.

To form the baklava, on wax paper stack 3 sheets of phyllo on top of each other, brushing liberally with butter between each sheet and on top. Cut the stack in half, crosswise, to create 2 smaller rectangles. Spread each rectangle with filling, leaving a 1-inch border around the edge. Fold the border along the longer sides of the rectangle in toward the center to hold the filling.

Tightly roll the pastry like a jelly roll, beginning at the short side. Set on a baking sheet and brush with butter.

Repeat this procedure to form 6 baklava. Bake the baklava at 350° until golden brown, cool.

To prepare the syrup, boil the granulated sugar with water, add mint and dried cherries until the cherries are tender. Lightly brush the baked baklava with this syrup.

Slice the baklava in half and set on serving plates. Serve with additional syrup and chocolate sauce, if desired.

SERVES: 6

 Wine Recommendation: Ridge Sonoma Zinfandel

Printer's Row restaurant is unique in its heritage of pioneering the revitalization of the Printer's Row neighborhood. The restaurant's main goal is to serve creative dishes with recipes based upon classic and contemporary American cuisine. Printer's Row and Executive Chef / Owner Michael Foley have won numerous regional, national, and international awards. Utilizing local ingredients where possible, Printer's Row continues to astonish its guests with an energetic staff in one of Chicago's most dynamic business locations.

Old Fashioned Apple Tart

INGREDIENTS

1½ cups all-purpose flour (pre-sifted)

½ tsp. salt

½ cup shortening (room temperature)

3 Tbs. water

4 large tart apples for baking

4 oz. butter

7 oz. sugar

4 egg yolks

9 oz. cream

pinch of cinnamon

Preheat oven to 425°.

Resift flour into a bowl with salt. With a pastry blender, work in shortening until the grain in the mixture is pea size.

Stir in water 1 Tbs. at a time, until the mixture holds together when you gather it into a ball. Roll dough on lightly floured surface to form a thin circle. Pat it evenly into the pie pan.

Bake tart pastry shell for 12 to 15 minutes. Cool before filling.

Peel and core the apples. Cut them into eighths. Heat a large skillet and add butter, the apples and 3 oz. of the sugar. Saute until cooked halfway. Remove apples, then add the remaining sugar and caramelize.

In a small bowl beat the egg yolks, cream and pinch of cinnamon. Arrange the apples in the shell, pour the caramel and egg mixture over the apples.

Bake at 400° for about 35 minutes.

SERVES: 8

Wine Recommendation: Schramsburg Cremant Sparkling Wine

A Gold Coast landmark for nearly 50 years, The Pump Room continues to attract the stars. Many celebrities frequent the restaurant and historical "Booth One" is still the place to be seated. The American cuisine is elegantly prepared by Executive Chef Brannon Soileau and the tradition of gracious dining, star gazing and excitement lives on. Don't forget to check out "Booth One."

Crispy Duck with Braised Red Cabbage

INGREDIENTS

Crispy Ducks:

2 whole ducks

3 sprigs of fresh thyme

4 stalks of celery

3 white onions, chopped & 2 carrots, sliced

Braised Red Cabbage:

2 red onions, sliced

2 green apples, cored & medium diced

1 head of red cabbage

½ cup red wine vinegar

1 cup (each) white and brown sugar

2 cups red wine

Cherry Sauce:

2 to 3 dried cherries

3 cups port wine & 1 cup red wine

Garlic Whipped Potatoes:

4 peeled & quartered potatoes

6 roasted garlic cloves

2 Tbs. heavy cream

2 Tbs. butter

Rinse duck under cold water. Rub with fresh thyme and salt & pepper.

Place the celery stalks, onions, and carrots in the bottom of a roasting pan. Lay the whole ducks, breast side down on the vegetables and place in 350° oven for 1 hour.

After 1 hour, turn ducks over showing the breast and cook another 15 minutes. Remove from oven and let cool. Once cool, remove the breast and leg. Let sit until ready for plate-up.

Saute red onions, apples and cabbage until wilted. Add vinegar, sugars and wine. Bring to a simmer and cover for 45 minutes. Adjust seasoning with salt & pepper. Let cool.

Soak the dried cherries in the port for 1 hour and then strain. In a sauce pan, reduce port and red wine down to a light syrup and hold warm.

Boil potatoes until tender and strain. Mash potatoes and garlic together. Add hot cream and butter until potatoes have a creamy texture. Season with salt & pepper to taste. Hold warm.

To serve, warm the duck in oven until hot, and then crisp the skin under the broiler.

Slice the duck breast into fans. Heat the red cabbage and circle around the potatoes. Rest the leg on the mashed potatoes and fan the sliced duck breast in front of the leg. Ladle the port sauce in front of the breast and drop the soaked cherries into the sauce.

SERVES: 4

Wine Recommendation: Estancia Merlot

Shaw's
CRAB HOUSE

Soft Shell Blue Crab with Mango

INGREDIENTS

4 - 8 soft shell crabs (dressed)

$\frac{1}{2}$ cup flour

$\frac{1}{4}$ cup melted unsalted butter

1 cup blanched spinach

1 large mango, diced in $\frac{1}{4}$ inch cubes

$\frac{1}{2}$ cup blanched red pepper, diced in $\frac{1}{4}$ inch pieces

$\frac{1}{4}$ cup diced jicama, diced in $\frac{1}{4}$ inch pieces

$\frac{1}{4}$ lb. butter

1 vanilla bean, split lengthwise

$\frac{1}{8}$ cup balsamic vinegar

salt & pepper to taste

To dress crabs, leave legs and claws on. Cut just below the eyes and remove face with scissors. Remove the gills and innards.

Place flour in large bowl and season with salt & pepper. Lightly coat crabs with flour, shaking off excess.

In a saucepan with the melted butter, saute crab over medium heat until brown (about 3-4 minutes per side). Set aside to drain.

Reheat spinach and form small bed in center of plate. Place crab on top and place 6 to 8 pieces of mango, red pepper, and jicama around.

To prepare sauce place a small pot on stove over medium high heat. Cut $\frac{1}{4}$ lb. butter into pieces and add to pot when pot is very hot. Butter should sizzle and brown immediately. Add vanilla bean and balsamic vinegar.

Ladle sauce over the crabs. Serve immediately.

SERVES: 4

 Wine Recommendation: Murphy Goode Reserve Fume Blanc

A Lincoln Park hot spot for over 10 years, Sole Mio serves regional Italian fare. The atmosphere is that of a romantic neighborhood trattoria with a comfortable friendly feel. Executive Chef / Owner Dennis Terczak provides guests with surroundings of oversized mirrors, parchment lamps and deep woods where diners feel at home in a suit or a pair of jeans.

Chocolate Caramel Custard

INGREDIENTS

2 cups sugar

½ cup water

3 cups milk

1 cup heavy cream

1 whole vanilla bean

1¼ oz. amaretto

¾ oz. of dark rum

1 oz. of cocoa

4 whole eggs

8 egg yolks

To make caramel, place 1 cup sugar and ½ cup water in sauce pan. Before heating, whisk sugar and water in pan to remove lumps. Heat the sugar and water without stirring until it caramelizes. Then pour into custard cups quickly.

To make the custard, mix the milk and heavy cream in a large saucepan. Add the other cup of sugar. Split vanilla bean, and scrape the inside into the milk mixture, discarding the shell. Heat this mixture until warm, stirring occasionally. Blend the amaretto, rum and cocoa into the warm mixture, then stir and scald the mixture until a thin skin forms on the surface (just before it erupts). Remove from heat.

Whisk the whole eggs and yolks together and then slowly whisk them into the milk mixture. Strain the whole mixture into a pitcher, then pour into cups over caramel mixture.

Preheat oven to 300°. Prepare a water bath by pouring hot or simmering water in a roasting pan and placing filled cups into the water bath. Don't let the water spill into cups. Cover the water bath with foil, shiny side up. Bake for 45 minutes to 1 hour. Check with a toothpick—if it stays up when inserted, they are done. Remove cups from water bath and let cool. Refrigerate until chilled.

SERVES: 8

 Wine Recommendation: Quady Essencia Orange Muscat

A lively addition to the Bucktown area, Soul Kitchen is a funky neighborhood restaurant that combines eclectic flavors with soul stirring music. Co-chefs Michael Clark and Monique King provide a menu utilizing seasonal ingredients and featuring bold flavors of the South, the Caribbean, Latin America and Asia. Soul Kitchen has been honored by several culinary publications and the restaurants motto of "loud food and spicy music" grooves on.

Paella "Jambalaya Style" in a Spicy Saffron Broth

INGREDIENTS

Spicy Saffron Broth:

1 Tbs. extra virgin olive oil

½ cup yellow onion, sliced

½ cup red bell pepper, sliced

½ tsp. garlic, chopped

1 jalapeno, sliced

½ tsp. saffron threads

1½ cups chicken broth

Saffron Risotto:

5 Tbs. extra virgin olive oil

1 medium onion, chopped

2½ cups Arborio rice

¾ cup white wine

6 cups chicken broth

1 tsp. saffron threads

salt to taste

Paella:

2 Tbs. extra virgin olive oil

½ cup red onion, sliced

1 Tbs. garlic, chopped

1 cup andouille sausage, sliced

1 cup chicken, diced

1 cup okra, sliced

1 lb. shrimp, cleaned, deveined, peeled

½ cup tomato, diced

1 lb. black mussels

To make the broth, heat the olive oil over low heat in a medium saucepan. Add onion, red pepper, garlic, jalapeno and saffron. Saute for 3 minutes. Add chicken broth and salt & pepper to taste. Simmer uncovered for 7 minutes. Reserve.

To make the risotto, heat the olive oil in a 4-quart saucepan over medium heat. Add onion and saute until soft. Add rice, mixing well until coated with oil. Add wine, stirring constantly over medium heat until wine evaporates. Add enough broth to cover the rice. Continue to stir until liquid is absorbed. Add broth a little at a time, constantly stirring until absorbed. Continue until all broth has been added and rice is cooked. Stir in saffron, add salt to taste. Reserve, covered.

To make the paella, heat olive oil in a large saucepan over low heat. Saute onion, garlic, andouille, chicken and okra for 7 minutes. Add shrimp, saute an additional 2 minutes.

Add reserved risotto and tomato; saute for 1 minute, mixing all ingredients. Add reserved saffron broth; bring to simmer.

Arrange mussels around the edge of the saute pan. Cover and steam for 5 minutes or until mussels open. Serve.

SERVES: 6

 Wine Recommendation: Meridian Chardonnay

Located in Chicago's burgeoning Bucktown neighborhood, Starfish serves eclectic American cuisine with Asian, Cajun, and Caribbean accents. Executive Chef Warren Long prepares creative menus that please a diverse clientele of chic locals and savvy suburbanites. The ambiance is intriguing, with stylish exposed-brick and an animated hip crowd.

Seared Jumbo Scallops & Vegetable Salad

INGREDIENTS

¼ cup of honey

½ cup of garlic chili sauce

1 cup of apple cider

¼ lb. of miso

1 yellow squash

1 eggplant

1 zucchini

1 lb. of lemongrass

1 tomato, diced

24 large scallops

Mix the honey, garlic chili sauce, apple cider and miso well. Set aside.

Cut all vegetables in half, then cut them on the bias. Roast the vegetables in oven at 350° for 10 minutes. Remove from oven and set aside.

To make the broth, place the lemongrass in 2 quarts of water. Bring to boil, then remove from heat. Remove the lemongrass from broth. Add diced tomatoes to broth and set aside.

Sear the scallops in a large skillet or on top of griddle for 2 minutes on each side.

Warm the vegetables and put in center of a serving plate. Place scallops around the vegetables. Ladle lemongrass broth over scallops and vegetables. Spoon miso sauce on top of each scallop. Garnish with chives or diced peppers.

SERVES: 4

Wine Recommendation: Gustav-Lorentz Pinot Blanc

Old Town favorite Topo Gigio serves wonderful Italian cuisine in a fun, light-hearted atmosphere. Restaurant Co-owner and Executive Chef Lillo Teodosi , born in Italy, prepares each meal with a "little bit of Rome." Topo Gigio has been a recipient of the annual International Food Manufactures award for Culinary Excellence for the past five years. Critically acclaimed in many culinary circles, Topo Gigio continues to shine.

Pan Roasted Chilean Sea Bass

INGREDIENTS

¹/₂ pt. yellow pear tomato, sliced lengthwise

1 small red onion, diced fine

1 tsp. tarragon, chopped fresh

¹/₂ green pepper, diced fine

¹/₂ red pepper, diced fine

2 Tbs. capers

1 oz. white balsamic vinegar

2 oz. olive oil

2 skinless Chilean sea bass (8 oz. each)

olive oil to coat pan

flour for dredging

salt & pepper to taste

To prepare vinaigrette, mix tomato, red onion, tarragon, green & red pepper, capers, vinegar, 2 oz. olive oil, and salt & pepper. Can be made up to 1 day ahead and kept refrigerated.

To prepare fish, pre-heat oven to 400°. Heat olive oil in saute pan. Dredge fillet in flour, shaking off excess. Sear fillet in pan and cook over moderate heat for 2 minutes.

Turn fish over and place in oven for 8 to 10 minutes or until golden brown.

To serve, place fish on plate and divide the vinaigrette on either side of fish. Serve with asparagus spears and new potatoes. Garnish with lemon wedge.

SERVES: 2

 Wine Recommendation: Cakebread Chardonnay

Un Grand Café

Un Grand Cafe is a lively, authentic Parisian bistro located in Lincoln Park. The atmosphere is elegantly casual and gives one the feeling of walking along the West Bank of Paris. Un Grand Cafe is part of a beautifully renovated old hotel and many admire its high ceilings and classic French doors. Executive Chef Ken Harris changes the menu weekly and treats guests to many innovative dishes.

Porcini Crusted Sauteed Salmon Steak

INGREDIENTS

1 oz. porcini powder

1 oz. flour

two 12 oz. salmon steaks

½ cup & 4 Tbs. olive oil

1 cup cleaned mixed greens

1 roasted red pepper, diced

2 oz. cleaned parsley

2 oz. cleaned chives

2 oz. cleaned basil

2 Tbs. toasted pine nuts

1 garlic clove

2 cups chicken broth

1 good punch of saffron

2 potatoes, diced

6 green beans, diced

3 tomatoes, diced

salt & pepper to taste

Mix the porcini powder and flour. Salt & pepper each side of salmon steak. Dust with porcini mix. Place in medium saute pan with 2 Tbs. olive oil. Cook till golden brown each side about 4 minutes. Remove fish.

In a clean saute pan, place 2 Tbs. olive oil with mixed greens. Season with salt & pepper. Add diced peppers. Mix for 1 minute until just wilted. Set aside.

To make sauce, place parsley chives, basil, ½ cup olive oil, pine nuts, garlic, salt & pepper in blender. Mix for 1 minute at high speed. Set aside,

Simmer chicken broth, saffron, potato, and salt & pepper until tender—about 3 minutes. Set aside.

Blanche green beans.

Place wilted greens in the center of the serving plate. Place yellow saffron potatoes around the plate. Place salmon steak on top of the wilted greens. Pour green herb sauce over salmon. Garnish salmon with diced green beans and tomatoes.

SERVES: 2

 Wine Recommendation: La Crema Pinot Noir

66

VINCI

A Lincoln Park favorite with the theater crowd, Vinci serves traditional Italian cuisine in a warm and casual environment. Executive Chef / Owner Paul LoDuca sets high standards for quality, while serving inventive interpretations of traditional Italian comfort foods. The decor is charming with large wall frescos from the work of Leonardo da Vinci.

Linguine della Nonna

INGREDIENTS

½ onion, diced

13 garlic cloves, peeled

9 oz. virgin olive oil

28 oz. can Italian tomatoes

1 cup stale bread, cut into small cubes

3 zucchini, cut in 1" slices

¼ tsp. red pepper flakes

1 cup chicken stock

1 lb. linguine, cooked al dente

salt & pepper to taste

To make the tomato concasse, sweat onions with 1 garlic clove and 2 oz. olive oil until the onions are transparent. Remove seeds and juice from can of tomatoes. Rough chop tomatoes and add to onion mixture. Bring to a boil, reduce heat and simmer until mixture is dry (about 20 minutes).

Preheat oven to 300°. Roast 12 garlic cloves in 4 oz. olive oil over low heat until golden brown and soft. Remove cloves from pan and set aside. Place bread into pan and saute until crispy, 2 - 3 minutes. Remove the bread and place into oven for 10 to 15 minutes, until dry and let cool.

Once bread cools, using flat side of a knife, crush bread until it is in crumbs and set aside.

Warm 3 oz. olive oil in pan and saute the zucchini until brown on both sides. Remove and set aside. Add pepper flakes and chicken stock to pan. Reduce by half. Toss garlic cloves, zucchini and linguine into the pan and quickly saute until well mixed.

Divide pasta into 4 portions and put in bowls. Top with tomato concasse and breadcrumbs.

SERVES: 4

 Wine Recommendation: St. Clement Sauvignon Blanc

YOSHI'S CAFÉ

A northside attraction, Yoshi's Cafe shines among Chicago's four-star eateries for its elegant and affordable meals. The restaurant serves classic French cuisine with a Japanese flair, as well as many creative European specialties. Chef Yoshi Katsumura and his wife and co-owner, Nobuko, revise the menu frequently and personally welcome guests at each table.

Veal Chop With Candied Lemon Zest And Ginger

INGREDIENTS

6 oz. fresh ginger root, peeled

zest of 3 lemons

1 cup water

1 cup sugar

7 - 10 shallots

1 quart Madeira (a sweet fortified wine)

2 cups veal stock (canned or frozen)

2 Tbs. butter

4 veal chops

1 Tbs. extra virgin olive oil

salt & pepper to taste

Julienne the ginger root and lemon zest by cutting them into match-stick-sized pieces. Blanch lemon zest and ginger in boiling water for 10 seconds. Set aside.

Bring 1 cup water and 1 cup sugar to a boil in saucepan. Reduce to a syrup. Add blanched ginger and lemon zest and cook for 5 minutes. Set aside.

Finely chop the shallots. Bring Madeira and shallots to a boil in a saucepan and reduce to a glaze. Add 2 cups veal stock to the Madeira and shallots. Reduce by half. Strain sauce, add salt and pepper to taste and 1 Tbs. butter to finish. Set aside.

Saute veal chops in 1 Tbs. butter and olive oil over medium high heat, approximately 3 - 4 minutes per side. Do not overcook. Veal chops should be medium rare to medium.

Remove veal chops to warm plates. Pour sauce around the chop and garnish with lemon zest and ginger.

Fried rice or fresh pasta is an excellent accompaniment.

SERVES: 4

Wine Recommendation: Turnbull Cabernet

Restaurant Locations

1. Arun's
   4156 North Kedzie Avenue
   Chicago, IL 60618
   773-539-1909

2. Berghoff
   17 West Adams Street
   Chicago, IL 60603
   312-427-3170

3. Bistro 110
   110 East Pearson
   Chicago, IL 60611
   312-266-3110

4. Blue Mesa
   1729 North Halsted Street
   Chicago, IL 60614
   312-944-5990

5. Brasserie Jo
   59 West Hubbard Street
   Chicago, IL 60610
   312-595-0800

6. Cafe Absinthe
   1958 West North Avenue
   Chicago, IL 60622
   773-278-4488

7. Cafe Bernard
   2100 North Halsted Street
   Chicago, IL 60614
   773-871-2100

8. Cafe Spiaggia
   980 North Michigan Avenue
   Chicago, IL 60611
   312-280-2750

9. Daniel J's
   3811 North Ashland Avenue
   Chicago, IL 60613
   773-404-7772

10. Dish
    3651 North Southport Avenue
    Chicago, IL 60613
    773-549-8614

11. Erwin
    2925 North Halsted Street
    Chicago, IL 60657
    773-528-7200

12. Everest
    One Financial Plaza, 40th Floor
    440 South La Salle Street
    Chicago, IL 60605
    312-663-8920

13. Green Dolphin Street
    2200 North Ashland Avenue
    Chicago, IL 60614
    773-395-0066

14. Havana Cafe Cubano
    230 West Kinzie Street
    Chicago, IL 60610
    312-595-0101

15. Hudson Club
    504 North Wells Street
    Chicago, IL 60610
    312-467-1947

16. Kiki's Bistro
    900 North Franklin Street
    Chicago, IL 60610
    312-335-5454

17. Le Bouchon
    1958 North Damen Avenue
    Chicago, IL 60647
    773-862-6600

18. Les Nomades
    222 East Ontario Street
    Chicago, IL 60611
    312-649-9010

19. Mango
    712 North Clark Street
    Chicago, IL 60610
    312-337-5440

20. Nick's Fishmarket
    One First National Plaza, lower level
    79 West Monroe Street
    Chicago, IL 60603
    312-621-0200

21. Papagus Greek Taverna
    620 North State Street
    Chicago, IL 60610
    312-642-8450

22. Printer's Row Restaurant
    550 South Dearborn Street
    Chicago, IL 60605
    312-461-0780

23. Pump Room
    1301 North State Parkway
    Chicago, IL 60610
    312-266-0360

24. Shaw's Crab House
    21 East Hubbard Street
    Chicago, IL 60611
    312-527-2722

25. Sole Mio
917 West Armitage Avenue
Chicago, IL 60614
773-477-5858

26. Soul Kitchen
1576 North Milwaukee Avenue
Chicago, IL 60622
773-342-9742

27. Starfish Cafe & Raw Bar
1856 West North Avenue
Chicago, IL 60622
773-395-3474

28. The Mashed Potato Club
316 West Erie
Chicago, IL 60610
312-255-8579

29. Topo Gigio Ristorante
1516 North Wells Street
Chicago, IL 60610
312-266-9355

30. Un Grand Cafe
2300 North Lincoln Park West
Chicago, IL 60614
773-348 8886

31. Vinci
1732 North Halsted Street
Chicago, IL 60614
312-266-1199

32. Yoshi's Cafe
3257 North Halsted Street
Chicago, IL 60657
773-248-6160

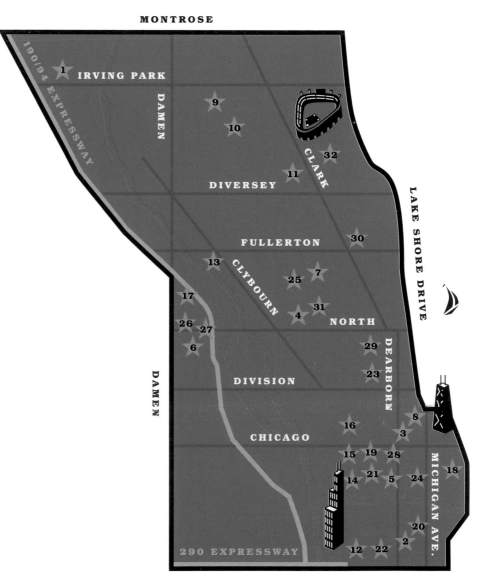

Glossary of Cooking Terms

-A-

Al dente - cooked pasta with chewy, not limp, consistency

Alsace Riesling - a steely, dry, highly aromatic wine

Allspice - berry of a Caribbean tree

Andouille - a mild, smoked pork sausage

Arborio - an Italian rice

Asiago - an Italian cheese

-B-

Baklava - sweet pastry made with phyllo dough and nuts

Balsamic vinegar - a sweet, dark rich vinegar

Basil - an herb

Bay leaf - the leaf of a laurel tree

Bias - to cut across on a slant or diagonal line

Blanch - to drop something into boiling water to tenderize

Blue cheese - fermented cheese

Bok choy - Chinese cabbage

Bouillabaisse - fish stew made with several kinds of fish

Braise - to cook meat in small amount of liquid in a covered container

Brandy - alcohol distilled from fermented fruit juice

Butternut squash - a light brown squash with sweet orange meat

-C-

Capers - pickled buds of a Mediterranean bush

Caraway seed - an annual herb

Cardamom - aromatic seeds from an Indian herb

Cayenne pepper - a chili pepper

Cheesecloth - meshed cotton cloth with a variety of cooking functions

Chive - a relative of the onion

Cilantro - a tangy green herb

Cherrystone clam - a young American clam

Clam juice - clam broth

Cloves - a pungy aromatic, dried bud

Coriander seed - dried seeds from a tangy green herb

Crabmeat - large clumps of solid white clam body meat

Cream - the fatty part of milk

Cream of tartar - a white powder from fermented wine barrels

Creme fraiche - a thick, flavorful form of matured cream

Cumin - an ancient spice

Currant - dried fruit of a small European grape

-D-

Demi glace - a rich, brown sauce made from beef stock, Madeira and brown sauce

Dredge - to lightly coat with flour, sugar, etc.

-F-

Fennel bulb - a plant used as a vegetable and an herb

Fold - to gently mix together

French flageolets - a small, dried bean of France

Fryer chicken - a young chicken

-G-

Genoise - a French sponge cake

Granny smith - a type of green apple

Green apple(s) - a tart apple, good for baking and cooking

-H-

Haricot vert - French green bean

-J-

Jalapeno - a hot Tex-Mex chili pepper

Jicama - a tropical root vegetable

Julienne - to cut into matchstick-sized pieces

Juniper - an aromatic dried berry

-L-

Leek - a sweet, mild onion flavored vegetable

Lemongrass - a tropical grass used in Asian cooking

-M-

Madeira - a sweet fortified wine

Mango - an fragrant tropical fruit

Marjoram - an herb similar to oregano

Mascarpone - a cream-style cheese

Mesclun - a salad of pot herbs

Mirepoix - mixture of carrot, onion, celery cooked in butter

Miso - fermented soybean paste

-N-

Nutmeg - spice made from the nut of an Oriental tree

-O-

Okra - fingerlike pod vegetable

Oyster mushroom - a soft, moist, peppery, shell-shaped mushroom

-P-

Paella - a Spanish specialty of rice with shellfish, chicken, and sausage

Porcini powder - ground dried porcini mushrooms

Parmesan - a hard, slightly sharp cheese

Phyllo dough - sheets of dough rolled thin and built up

Pine nut - edible seed that grows in pine cones

Pistachio - a greenish, almondlike nut

Porcini - a dome-shaped mushroom

Port - a fortified wine

Portabella - a large, brown, beefy mushroom

Puree - to run cooked food through a blender or food processor

-R-

Reduce - to boil down

Rhubarb - a tart field plant

Rosemary - a Mediterranean herb

Roux - equal parts of flour and butter to thicken a sauce

-S-

Saffron - threadlike flower parts from a purple-flowered crocus

Sage - an aromatic gray-green leafed herb

Savory - a spice

Sear - cook something on high heat to form a crust on the outside or to enhance flavor

Shallot - a small member of the onion family

Star anise - a star-shaped, eight-point herb

Stockpot - a large cooking pot for making soups and stocks

-T-

Tahini - a spread made from ground sesame seeds

Tarragon - an aromatic herb

Terrine - a small earthenware dish

-V-

Venison - the meat of deer

-W-

Worcestershire sauce - a thin, dark sauce

-Z-

Zest - the rind of a lemon, orange, lime, etc...

Zucchini - part of the squash family

Index

-A-

Amaretto 24, 58
Andouille 60
Apple(s)
    granny smith 28
    green 54
    tart apples. 52
Apple cider. 28, 62

-B-

Bacon. 40, 42
Baklava. 50
Banana. 44
Bass, sea bass 30, 64
Beans
    black 46
    French flageolets 16
    green 66
    haricot vert 22
    string 16, 22
Beef cutlet 10
Beef stock 10
Berries 26, 32
Bisque. 28
Bisquick 26
Bok choy 8
Bouillabaisse. 30
Brandy 22
Bread
    breadcrumbs. 48, 68
Bread Pudding. 24
Buttermilk 26

-C-

Cabbage, red 54
Caper(s) 64
Caramel 24, 52
    Chocolate caramel custard 58
Champagne 26
Cheese
    asiago 32
    blue cheese 36
    goat 20

    mascarpone 32
    parmesan 32
Cheesecloth. 32, 48
Cherries, dried 50, 54
Chicken 8, 28, 60
    chicken bones 38
    chicken broth 60, 66
    fryer 38
    stock 32, 38, 42, 68
Chili sauce, garlic 62
Chocolate
    caramel custard. 58
    white chocolate 14
Chowder, clam caraway 42
Chutney 32
Clam(s)
    cherrystone clams 42
    juice 30, 42
Corn meal, blue. 26
Crab(s), crabcakes 48
    crabmeat. 48
    soft shell, blue 56
Cream. 42, 52
    heavy cream 12, 40, 54, 58
Creme fraiche 18, 26
Currant(s). 32
Custard 24, 58

-D-

Dacqoise. 44
Duck 54

-E-

Egg(s) . . . 8, 14, 22, 24, 40, 44, 48, 50, 58
Eggplant. 62

-F-

Fennel bulb 30
Feulliuetine flakes 44
Fish
    crabmeat. 48
    monk fish 30
    red snapper 30, 34
    sea bass 30, 64
    soft shell crab 56

    stock 30, 48
    tuna. 12

-G-

Genoise. 44
Greens, mixed 66

-H-

Herb(s)d'Provence 38
Honey. 14, 32, 62
Hummus 46

-J-

Jalapeno 8, 34, 60
Jambalaya 60
Jicama 56
Juniper 32

-K-

Kahlua 24

-L-

Lamb, shank(s) 16
Leek. 30
Lemon 64
    juice. 22, 24, 44, 46, 48
    zest. 70
Lemongrass 62
Lettuce, frisse 36
Linguine 68

-M-

Madeira 10, 70
Mango. 56
Marinade 8, 20
    jerked 34
Mayonnaise. 22, 48
Milk 24, 42, 58
Mirepoix 32
Miso. 62
Mojo 34
Monk fish 30
Mousse. 14, 44
Mushroom(s)
    crimini. 12
    oyster. 12

porcini 66
portabella 12, 20
Mussels, black 60

-O-

Okra 60
Onion
    red 18, 34, 54, 60, 64
    tart 40
Ostrich 18

-P-

Paella 60
Pear, Asian 36
Pepper
    green bell 48, 64
    red bell 48, 56, 60, 64, 66, 68
Peppercorn(s) 38
    green 32
    pink 12
Phyllo dough 50
Pickle 10
Pine nut(s) 66
Pistachio 50
Porcini 66
Potato
    Idaho 12
    whipped 54

-Q-

Quesadilla 14

-R-

Raspberry 14
    liqueur 14
Red snapper 30, 34
Rhubarb 32
Rice
    Arborio 60
    jasmine 32
    noodles 8

-S-

Saffron 30, 44, 66
    broth 60
    risotto 60

Salad
    Asian pear 36
    Strawberry red onion 18
Salmon steak 66
Salsa 34, 46
Sausage, andouille 60
Sea bass, Chilean 30, 64
Sea scallop(s) 30
Shallot(s) 16, 20, 48, 70
Shortcake(s) 26
Shrimp 22, 30, 60
Sour cream 28
Spinach 20, 56
Sponge Cake 44
Squash
    butternut 28
    yellow 62
Star anise 32
Stir fry 8
Stock
    beef 10
    chicken 8, 28, 32, 42, 68
    fish 30, 48
    veal 32, 38, 70
Sugar 8, 14, 18, 24, 26, 36
    . . . . 44, 50, 52, 58, 70
    brown 28, 34, 54
    powdered 14, 44

-T-

Tahini 46
Tarragon 64
Tart
    apple 52
    onion 40
Terrine 30
Thyme 16, 20, 30, 32, 34, 38, 42, 54
    wild 38
Tomato
    concasse 68
    Italian 68
    mojo 34
    yellow pear 64
Tortilla(s) 14, 18
Tuna, yellow-fin 12

-V-

Vanilla 14, 24
    bean 56, 58
Veal
    chop 70
    ground 10
    stock 32, 38, 70
Venison 32
Vinegar
    balsamic 12, 18, 20, 56, 64
    jalapeno 8
    red wine 32, 54
    rice wine 36
    sherry wine 36
    tarragon 64
    white balsamic 64

-W-

Walnut 36
Wine
    Alsace Riesling 16
    port 54
    red 32, 54
    white 32, 38, 48, 60
Worcestershire sauce 12

-Z-

Zest
    lemon 70
    lime 48
    orange 48
Zucchini 62, 68

Conversion Chart

Weights and Measures

1 pinch = less than $\frac{1}{8}$ tsp.

3 tsp. = 1 Tbs. = $\frac{1}{2}$ oz.

2 Tbs. = 1 oz.

4 Tbs. = $\frac{1}{4}$ cup

1 cup = 8 fl. oz.

$\frac{1}{2}$ cup = 4 fl. oz.

1 quart = 2 pints

Equivalents

8 Tbs. = 4 oz. = $\frac{1}{2}$ cup = 1 stick butter

1 large egg = 2 oz. = $\frac{1}{4}$ cup = 4 Tbs.

1 egg yolk = 1 Tbs. + 1 tsp.

1 egg white = 2 Tbs. + 2 tsp.

Temperatures

205 degrees Fahrenheit - water simmers

212 degrees Fahrenheit - water boils

350 degrees Fahrenheit - baking

400 degrees Fahrenheit - hot oven

450 degrees Fahrenheit - very hot oven

500 degrees Fahrenheit - broiling

Notes

Notes